Key skills for kids
ENGLISH

Let's get started!

priddy books
big ideas for little people

Contents

Write letters A–M	4	More short vowels	36
Write letters A–M	5	Problem and solution	37
Write letters N–Z	6	Predict	38
Write letters N–Z	7	Write the ending	39
Nature abc	8	Adjectives	40
All about me	9	Adjectives	41
Days of the week	10	Shape poems	42
Days of the week	11	Shape poems	43
What is 'I'?	12	Beginning blends	44
Characters	13	Beginning blends	45
Create a character	14	More beginning blends	46
Compare characters	15	Retell	47
Setting	16	Main topic	48
Characters and setting	17	Sort words	49
Capital letters	18	Tricky words	50
Punctuation	19	More tricky words	51
Use punctuation	20	Nouns	52
Sentences	21	Proper nouns	53
Beginning sounds	22	Possessive noun	54
Ending sounds	23	Making connections	55
Spelling patterns	24	Final blends	56
Spelling patterns	25	Final blends	57
More spelling patterns	26	Fairy tales	58
Look at the picture	27	Multiple-meaning words	59
Fiction or non-fiction	28	Personal pronouns	60
Key details	29	Pronouns	61
Sequence events	30	Question words	62
Short vowel 'a'	31	Question words	63
Short vowel 'e'	32	Ask and answer questions	64
Short vowel 'i'	33	'A', 'an' and 'the'	65
Short vowel 'o'	34	Digraphs	66
Short vowel 'u'	35	Digraphs	67

Verbs	68
Verb tenses	69
Nearly the same	70
Silent 'e'	71
How to	72
How to	73
Long vowel 'a'	74
Long vowel 'e'	75
Long vowel 'i'	76
Long vowel 'o'	77
Long vowel 'u'	78
Long vowels	79
Time words	80
Using time words	81
Syllables	82
Syllables	83
Long or short vowels	84
The letter 'y'	85
Singular and plural nouns	86
Nouns and verbs	87
Finding clues	88
Finding clues	89
Make an inference	90
Position	91
3-letter blends	92
3-letter blends	93
Plan a non-fiction text	94
Write a non-fiction text	95
Which letter is saying its name?	96
Which letter is saying its name?	97
Compound words	98
Point of view	99
Author's point	100
Split digraphs	101
Joining words	102
Joining words	103
Extended sentences	104
Tricky words	105
Root words	106
Suffixes	107
'Er', 'est'	108
'Tch'	109
'Air' and 'ear'	110
Prefixes and suffixes	111
Make a timeline	112
Plan a narrative	113
Make a draft	114
Write a narrative	115
Write an opinion	116
Write a letter	117

Answers are on pages 118–127!

Write letters A–M

Uppercase letters are also called **capital letters**.

There are 26 letters in the alphabet. Each letter can be written in **uppercase** and **lowercase**.

1 Trace and write the capital and lowercase letters.

A A A	**a** a a
B B B	**b** b b
C C C	**c** c c
D D D	**d** d d
E E E	**e** e e

F F F

f f f

G G G

g g g

H H H

h h h

I I I

i i i

J J J

j j j

K K K

k k k

L L L

l l l

M M M

m m m

Write letters N–Z

Can you think of any words that begin with these letters?

1 Trace and write the capital and lowercase letters.

N NN	**n** nn
O OO	**o** oo
P PP	**p** pp
Q QQ	**q** qq
R RR	**r** rr

S SS

s ss

T TT

t tt

U UU

u uu

V VV

v vv

W WW

w ww

X XX

x xx

Y YY

y yy

Z ZZ

z zz

Nature abc

1 Fill in the missing lowercase letters.

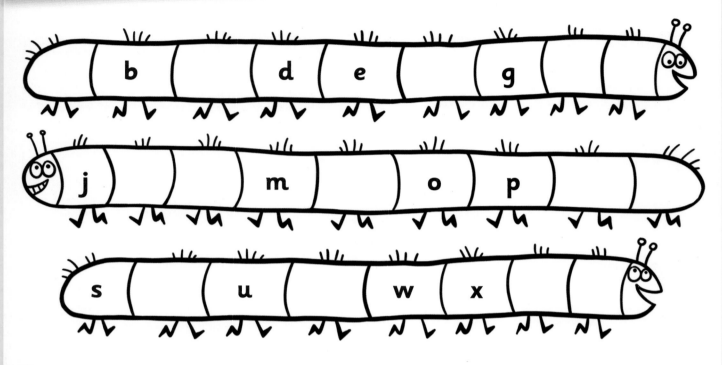

| b | | | d | e | | g | |

| j | | | m | | o | p | | |

| s | | | u | | w | x | | |

2 Following the example, write the words in **alphabetical order** on the lines below.

moth   ant   snail   bee

1. ....ant.............

2. ....

3. ....

4. ....

Use the first letter of each word to help put them in abc order.

All about me

1 Write your first name and last name. Then draw a picture of yourself in the frame.

Don't forget to use a capital letter for the first letter of your first name and your last name.

My name is

....

....

2 Answer each question.

My favourite food is

....

My favourite colour is

....

My birthday is in the month of

....

Days of the week

There are seven days in a week.

Days of the week always start with a **capital letter**.

1 Read the days of the week aloud.

Monday	Tuesday	Wednesday

Thursday	Friday	Saturday	Sunday

2 Following the example, write which day comes next.

Tuesday / Wednesday / Thursday — Friday

Sunday / Monday / Tuesday — ....

Thursday / Friday / Saturday — ....

3 Fill in the chart with the correct days of the week.

Yesterday	Today	Tomorrow
Tuesday	Wednesday	
	Monday	
	Sunday	
	Thursday	

Adam's diary

Adam does a different activity on each day of the week.

Monday	Tuesday	Wednesday	Thursday	Friday

Swim lesson	Piano lesson	Park	Football game	Party

1 Which day does Adam do each activity? Write the day in the correct place in the crossword.

Use the pictures to help you!

What is 'I'?

'I' can be a letter or a word.

Always use a **capital letter** when writing 'I' as a word.

1 Read the text.
Circle the word 'I' in each sentence.

I like bears.
I like parrots.
I like monkeys.
I do not like snakes!

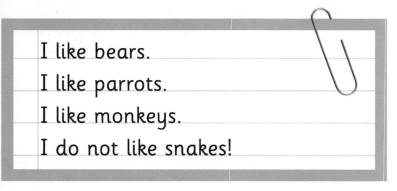

2 Colour the word 'I' pink.
Colour the word '**me**' green.

Characters

Characters are the people, animals or creatures in a story.

1 Put an **X** next to the pictures that are characters.

2 Complete the sentences.

My favourite book is

....

The characters in the book are

....

Create a character

Every story has a **main character**. The main character is the person or animal that the story is mostly about.

1 Create a character by filling in the blanks.

Argh! I'm Captain Toby, a scary pirate.

My character's name is ....
My character lives in ....
My character likes to ....

2 Circle three words that describe your character.

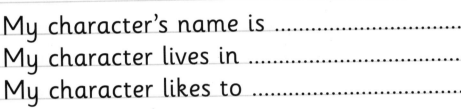

kind	noisy	bossy	brave	clumsy
happy	wild	loving	shy	funny

3 Draw a picture of your character, then write their description.

14

Compare characters

Compare means to find things that are similar or different.

Readers can compare characters in a story.

1 Read the story below.

Tom and May sat down to eat lunch.
Tom opened his lunch box. "Yes, I love my lunch!"
May opened her lunch box. "Oh no!" she said.
Tom started to eat his fruit. He saw that May was sad.
"Do you want some grapes?" he asked.
May smiled. "Yes, please," she said.
"I have strawberries, but I don't
like them." "I like strawberries!" said Tom.
May and Tom shared their grapes
and strawberries.

2 Tick the phrases that are true for each character.

	May	Tom
Likes strawberries		
Does not like strawberries		
Shares lunch with a friend		

Setting

A **setting** is where and when a story takes place.

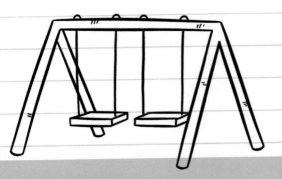

1 Draw a line to match the characters to their settings.

Three Little Pigs

Humpty Dumpty

Little Red Riding Hood

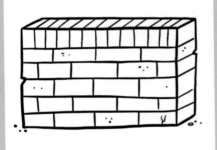

2 Tick the pictures that show where a story can take place.

school

duck

pond

tree house

Characters and setting

The **characters** and **setting** are details that help readers understand the story.

1. Read the story. Then circle the character names.

> Goose and Duck are best friends. They live in the same pond.
> They love to play together every day.
> One day, Goose and Duck saw black dots by their pond.
> The next day the black dots were gone!
> Lots of new frog friends had come to live and play with them.

2. Can you label the characters in the picture?

Label means to write the word next to the picture that relates to it.

3. Where did the story take place? ....

Capital letters

Days, months and names begin with a capital letter.

Capital letters are used at the start of a sentence.

1   Underline the words that need a capital letter.

| december | sunday | john | dog |

| car | august | jump | mary |

2   Circle the capital letters in each sentence.

a. We jumped so high.
b. My best friend is Cleo.
c. No way!
d. Are you going to play basketball on Friday?

3   Write out each sentence with capital letters in the correct places.

a. the kangaroo loves to jump.

....

b. his name is hopper.

....

Hello, I'm Hopper!

c. can you jump higher than he can?

.... ?

18

Punctuation

Every sentence has spaces between the words and **punctuation** to mark the end of the sentence. Some of the punctuation marks we use are **.** **?** or **!**

1 Draw a line from each punctuation mark to its name.

?   **!**   **.**

exclamation mark   full stop   question mark

2 Tick the sentence with the correct punctuation in each pair.

full stop

- [ ] I am. seven years old
- [ ] My name is Harvey.

An **exclamation** is a sentence that shows strong feelings or excitement.

question mark

- [ ] Where is the party**?**
- [ ] Can you teach me **?** how to play

exclamation mark

- [ ] Happy birthday**!**
- [ ] **!** Wow

Use punctuation

1. Add the correct punctuation to the end of each sentence.

Remember to use a . ? or !

a. We like to play football ......

b. Where is your cat ......

c. This is so exciting ......

d. What is your favourite colour ......

e. Watch out for the swing ......

f. I can climb the tree ......

2. Write the words below in order so that the sentence makes sense.

| many | ? | kittens | How | do | have | you |

....

Sentences

Sentences begin with a capital letter and end with a **.** **?** or **!**

---

1 Rewrite each sentence using a capital letter and a **.** **?** or **!**

a. can you juggle ....

b. i want a red balloon ....

c. oh no ....

2 Write two sentences about the picture.

1. ....
   ....
   ....
   ....

2. ....
   ....
   ....
   ....

Use a capital letter at the beginning and a **.** **?** or **!** at the end of each sentence.

Beginning sounds

A **beginning sound** is the first sound heard in a word.

1 Write the beginning sound for each of the pictures below.

 b̲ird

 ......izza

 ......indow

 ......uice

Say each word aloud first.

2 Complete the crossword puzzle by writing the beginning sounds.

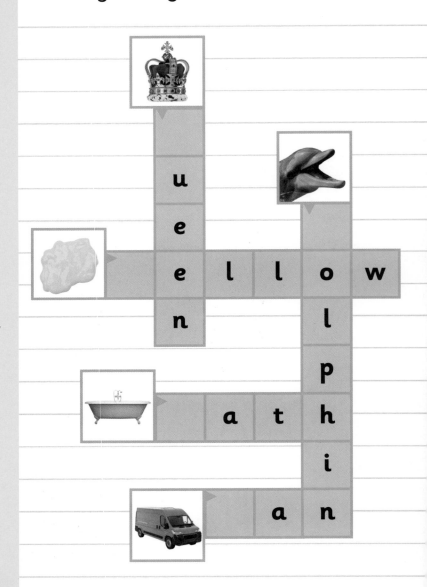

End sounds

An **end sound** is the last sound heard in a word.

1 Circle the correct end sound for each of the pictures.

  **(n)** m h

 q p b

 d p b

 h d b

 s v f

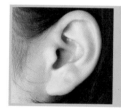 r e l

2 Write the end sound for each of the pictures below.

 lam......

 bu......

 ne......

 gir......

23

Spelling patterns

A **spelling pattern** is a group of letters that make a special sound when they are put together.

Spelling patterns are sometimes called **word families**.

1 Draw a line to match words with the '**ag**' spelling pattern to the correct picture.

flag	bag	wag

 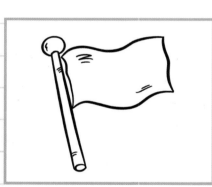 

2 Finish writing each word with the '**an**' spelling pattern.

 m............

 p............

 f...........

 r...........

3 The words below have an '**ell**' or '**ill**' spelling pattern. Read each word aloud.

	ill		shell
	bell		hill
	spill		drill
	well		yell

4 Sort each word from Activity 3 into the correct group.

'ell'	'ill'
....	....
....	....
....	....
....	....

More spelling patterns

1 Circle the words with the '**op**' spelling pattern.

Spelling patterns can help you to spell new words.

bed	(stop)	pop
mop	clock	hop

2 Use the '**ug**' spelling pattern to write the words.

 r...........

 b...........

 m...........

 j...........

3 Choose an '**ug**' word from the word bank to fill in the gaps.

1. Miles pulled the .... out of the sink.

2. Natalie .... a hole in the sand.

Word bank

dug
plug

Look at the picture

Pictures give a clue about what is happening in the story.

Pictures can also be called **illustrations**.

1 Look at the picture.
Write a story about what is happening in the picture.

....
....
....
....
....
....
....
....

2 Read the beginning of the story below. Draw a picture to match.

Anna is excited to be at the funfair. She can't wait to go on the fast ride.

Fiction or non-fiction

Fiction texts come from our imaginations, they are often full of magic and make-believe. **Non-fiction** texts are true. They give information.

1 Read the title of each book. Draw a line to show whether it is a fiction or non-fiction text.

Fiction　　　　**Non-fiction**

2 Read the sentences.
Write **F** next to the sentences from a fiction text.
Write **N** next to the sentences from a non-fiction text.

a. The monster jumped on the bed. ☐

b. Bees have six legs. ☐

c. Animals need food and water to survive. ☐

d. The princess kissed the frog. ☐

Key details

Key details are important pieces of information in a text.

1 Read the text about the life cycle of a frog.

A frog lays tiny eggs in the water. Tadpoles hatch from the eggs.
Tadpoles look like little fish with long tails.
Tails help the tadpoles swim.

When tadpoles grow legs, they are called froglets.
Froglets look like little frogs with tails.

As the froglets grow, their tails get shorter.
Then froglets become frogs.

2 Label the life cycle of a frog by choosing the correct word.

frog	froglet	eggs	tadpole

1

4

2

3

....

....

....

....

Sequence events

Sequence events means to put different parts of a story in order of when they happen.

1 Read the story.

On Sunday, it was hot outside. Dad took me to the park.
We took my dog, Chip, with us. I got strawberry ice cream.
When Chip saw a squirrel, he started to run away.
I jumped and my ice cream fell! I was sad.
Then Dad shared his chocolate ice cream with me.

2 Put the story in the correct order by writing 1, 2 or 3 in the boxes.

3 Cross out the word that does not describe the setting of the story.

| outside | park | Sunday | school |

Short vowel 'a'

Vowels can make many sounds. The same letter can sound long or short, depending on the word that it is in.

The short 'a' vowel sounds like /a/ in the word 'cat'.

1 Say each word aloud. Fill in the space with the vowel 'a'. Then write each word.

 m.......p
....

 r.......t
....

 cr.......b
....

 s.......d
....

2 Read each word aloud.
Circle the words that have the short 'a' sound.

dad	mop	bad	cab	hut
that	has	leaf	mat	book

Short vowel 'e'

The short 'e' vowel sounds like /e/ in the word '**bed**'.

1 Say each word aloud.
Fill in the space with the
vowel '**e**'. Then write each word.

10 t.......n

....

n.......st

....

r.......d

....

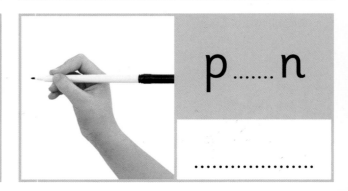
p.......n

....

2 Read each word aloud. Draw a line from the
words that have a short '**e**' sound to the circle.

bed

get

boot

car

short 'e'

face

cape

men

branch

Short vowel 'i'

1   Read each word with the short 'i' sound.
    Then write each word under its matching picture.

| six | fish | pig | twins |

....

2   Read each word aloud.
    Tick the words with the short 'i' sound.

☐ **big**   ☐ **win**   ☐ **lip**

☐ **plane**   ☐ **his**   ☐ **brake**

☐ **dirt**   ☐ **dress**   ☐ **fin**

Short vowel 'o'

The short 'o' vowel sounds like /o/ in the word '**hot**'.

1 Read each short '**o**' word aloud.
Write each word under the correct picture.

box	stop	sock

 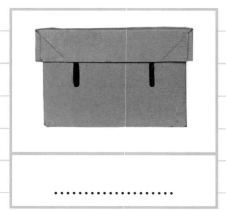 

....

2 Draw a line from each short '**o**' word to the correct picture.

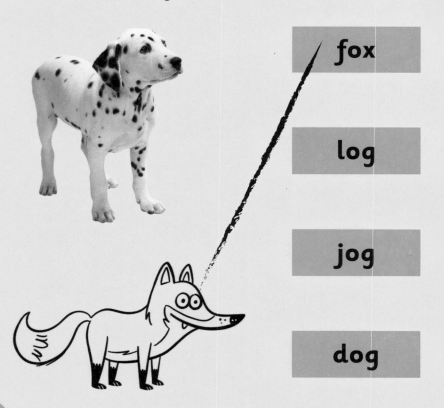

fox

log

jog

dog

Short vowel 'u'

The short 'u' vowel sounds like /u/ in the word '**bug**'.

1 Unscramble the letters to make a word with the short '**u**' sound.

t c u

....

u c p

....

t u n

....

u g h

....

2 Find the short '**u**' words in the word search.

☐ **cub**

☐ **drum**

☐ **duck**

☐ **fun**

☐ **jug**

Tick the words off as you find them!

f	u	n	h	d	j
b	d	r	u	m	c
a	u	j	d	j	w
y	c	f	w	u	h
b	k	s	q	g	i
i	a	i	c	u	b
e	d	k	x	z	g

More short vowels

Remember the short vowels are 'a', 'e', 'i', 'o' and 'u'.

1 Write the correct short vowel sound to complete the word.

h......t

p......p

c......t

n......ck

w......g

p......t

h......p

p......g

j......t

n......t

dr......m

b......t

Problem and solution

Most stories include a problem and a solution.
A **problem** is something a character wants to fix or figure out. A **solution** is how the problem is fixed or solved.

1 Read the text.

Arzo got a skateboard for his birthday.
He stood up on the skateboard but fell down again.

Mum said, "Arzo, let's watch some videos and
learn how to ride." Arzo and Mum watched
videos and practised all week.

By the end of the week, Arzo was able to ride
his skateboard. "You did it!" Mum cheered.

2 Answer the following questions.

1. What is the problem?

....

....

2. What is the solution to the problem?

....

....

Predict

Predict means making a good guess about what will happen.

Good readers make **predictions** before and while reading a text.

1 Look at the picture on the cover of the book. Predict what the book will be about.

I predict that the book will be about

....

....

2 Look at the pictures from the middle of a different book. Predict what will happen next.

I predict that

....

....

Write the ending

The **ending** of a story usually includes a solution to the problem.

1 Read the text.

The Brown family went on a trip to the beach. It was a long trip, so Dad drove while Mum, Kia and Kevin went to sleep. Dad drove and drove.
After a while, Dad woke up his family.
He said, "Oh no! I think we are lost."

2 What happens next?
Write an ending for the story.

Make sure you tell how the Brown family solves their problem.

....
....
....
....
....
....
....
....
....
....

Adjectives

Adjectives are describing words that tell us more about a person, place or thing.

1 Circle the describing words.

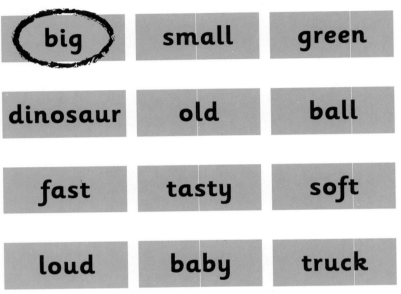

(big) small green

dinosaur old ball

fast tasty soft

loud baby truck

I am a **big** monster!

2 Choosing from the words below, write the adjective that best describes each dinosaur picture.

spotty   spiky   tiny

....

....

....

3 Write a word to describe each picture underneath it.

....

....

....

4 Read the adjectives in the word bank aloud.
   Then add in the adjectives to complete the story.

Word bank

yellow
shiny
~~cold~~
new
blue

It was a ......cold...... night. Mum told Dino
to put on his .... jacket.
"No! I want to wear my .... raincoat,"
said Dino. "I like my .... raincoat the best."
"Okay," said Mum. "Make sure you wear
your .... wellies, too."

5 Circle the adjective in each sentence.

a. The dinosaur walked across the green grass.
b. That is a beautiful waterfall.
c. Some dinosaurs ate leaves from tall trees.
d. Some dinosaurs had pointy teeth.

41

A **shape poem** is a poem in the shape of an object. The words and phrases used in the poem usually describe that object.

1 Read the shape poem about pizza.

Soft golden crust.
Ooey-gooey yellow cheese.
Sweet, juicy pineapple.
Spicy sauce, please!
Get it while it's hot.
Perfect pizza.
Munch!
Yum!

2 Which words from the pizza poem relate to the five senses? Write them below.

3 Write a shape poem about ice cream. Use words or phrases to describe ice cream in your poem.

....
....
....
....
....
....

....
....
....
....
....
....
....
....

Use some words that connect to your five senses.

4 Which words in your ice cream poem connect to the five senses? Write them below.

Sight	Touch	Sound	Smell	Taste
....	....	....	....	....

Beginning blends

Blends are two or three letters that keep their own sounds when put together.

Blends can be at the **beginning** of a word.

1 Colour in the correct beginning blend for each picture.

 **gl** **fl**

cl **gl**

 **bl** **pl**

 **bl** **pl**

 **cl** **gl**

 **cl** **fl**

 **pl** **gl**

 **pl** **fl**

2 Can you match each of these words to an example?

plus	gloves	black	climb

Something to keep your hands warm		Go up using your hands and feet	
gloves	....	....	....

44

3 Choose the correct '**br**' or '**pr**' blend for each word.

..........oom

..........esent

..........ice

..........ead

..........ush

..........ize

4 Choose the correct '**gr**' or '**cr**' blend for each word.

..........ab

..........ane

..........een

..........apes

..........ow

..........in

More beginning blends

1 Fill in the correct blend to complete the words.

| sc | sn | ~~sp~~ | sw |

 ..sp..onge

 ....ing

 ....ail

 ....arf

2 Choose the correct blend to fill in the gaps.

 I can ..sm..ell the ..sk..unk.

(sm)/sw   sl/(sk)

 I like to ride my ....ooter.

sc/sn

I like to ride my ....ooter.

Do you know how to ....i in the ....ow?

sk/st   sm/sn

Try each blend out first.

46

Retell

Retell means to tell the important parts of the story, including characters, setting, beginning, middle and end.

1 Read the text.

Jo and Akim went to the park to play football.
Akim brought his ball. They started to play.
Jo took a shot at the goal. She kicked the ball hard.
Oh no! The ball shot over the fence and into a garden.
Akim ran to the fence. A man was in the garden.
He picked up the ball and gave it to Akim.
"Thank you," said Akim. Happily, Jo and Akim began to play again.

2 Who are the characters?

1. ....
2. ....
3. ....

3 Where is the setting?

....

....

4 Write what happened at the beginning, in the middle and at the end of the story.

Beginning	Middle	End
....	....	....
....	....	....
....	....	....
....	....	....
....	....	....

Main topic

The **main topic** describes what the text is mostly about.

1 Read the text.

Plants have many parts. Each plant part has a special job.
Roots hold the plant in the ground. They help plants
get water and food to live.
The **stem** holds the plant up. It also helps carry
water and food through the plant.
The **leaves** use water, air and sunlight to make food.
The **flowers** bring insects that help the plant grow seeds.
The **seeds** can grow into new plants.

2 What is the main topic of the text? Circle the correct answer.

a. Animal parts

b. Plant parts

c. Body parts

Check the text for your answer.

3 Use the bold words from the text to help label the parts of a plant.

flower

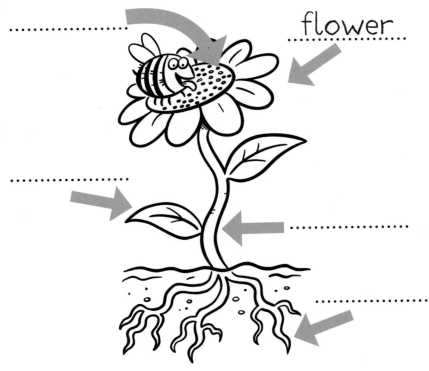

Sort words

Words can be sorted into **groups** or categories.

1 Write each word in the correct group.

piano	doll	violin	robot
drum	ball	flute	teddy bear

Toys	Instruments

2 Read the words in each group.
Write a name to describe each group.

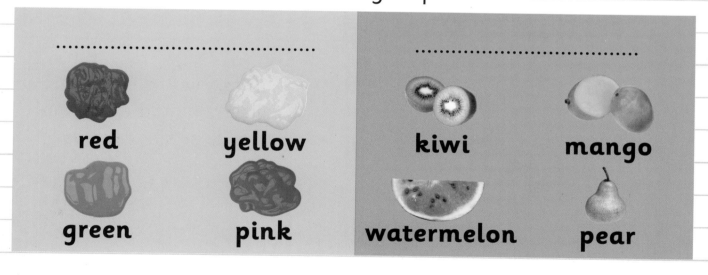

....

red   yellow   kiwi   mango

green   pink   watermelon   pear

3 Write four words for the category '**clothes**'.

....

....

Tricky words

Tricky words are common words found in text. They should be recognised quickly by sight.

1 Read and trace each tricky word.
   Then write each word in two colours.

Read the word	Trace the word	Write the word in two different colours
of	of	of of
give	give	
put	put	
were	were	

2 Find each of the tricky words in the word search.

Tricky words are also called common exception words or sight words.

p	w	e	r	e	g
x	v	o	p	w	i
m	p	u	t	g	v
g	y	v	o	f	e

☐ of
☐ give
☐ put
☐ were

More tricky words

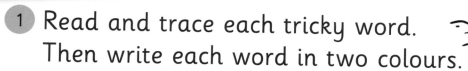

1. Read and trace each tricky word.
   Then write each word in two colours.

Read the word	Trace the word	Write the word with two different colours
her	her	
walk	walk	
again	again	
know	know	

2. Circle the correct letters to spell each tricky word.

her	m (h) i a (e) (r) f s
walk	w i a c l k c
again	a j g a l i n m
know	l k t n o u w x

Nouns

A **noun** is a person, animal, place or thing.

1. Are each of these pictures a person, animal, place or thing? Tick the correct box.

school

- ☐ person
- ☐ animal
- ☐ place
- ☐ thing

desk

- ☐ person
- ☐ animal
- ☐ place
- ☐ thing

hamster

- ☐ person
- ☐ animal
- ☐ place
- ☐ thing

teacher

- ☐ person
- ☐ animal
- ☐ place
- ☐ thing

2. Circle the nouns.

nurse	jump
book	play
pencil	boy
dog	run
office	glue
look	bird
flag	cry
cat	park

3. Circle the nouns in each sentence. Some sentences have two nouns.

a. The girl ate pizza.

b. The bell rang loudly.

c. A bus is coming.

d. There are five fish in the bowl.

Proper nouns

A **proper noun** names a specific person, place or thing.

For example, New York is a proper noun. It is the name of a city.

> Proper nouns need a capital letter.

1 Circle all the proper nouns.

city	Mrs Jones	Scotland	chocolate
woman	Europe	rat	Hannah

2 Fill in the chart by writing a proper noun next to each common noun.

Common noun	Proper noun
month	October
boy	
country	
planet	
city	

Word bank

October
Mars
Jack
London
Spain

3 Write your name, the town and the country where you live. Remember to use a capital letter at the beginning of each word.

1. ....

2. ....

3. ....

Possessive nouns

A **possessive noun** shows ownership of a person, place or thing. To show ownership, add an apostrophe ' and the letter '**s**'. For example, 'Kim**'s** bike' shows a possessive noun.

1 Choose a noun from the word bank to finish each sentence. Add **'s** to make the noun possessive.

| car | Tara | tiger | bird |

.... toy is broken.

The .... nest is filled with eggs.

The .... tyre is flat.

The .... stripes are beautiful.

Making connections

Making connections means learning how things are related. Readers can make connections between people, events and information in a text.

1 Read the text.

Turtles and tortoises

Many people think a turtle and a tortoise are the same.
They are both reptiles with shells, but they are not the same.
A turtle lives in the water. A tortoise lives on land.
They both lay their eggs on land.
A turtle has a light flat shell. A tortoise has a heavy round shell.
They have different feet, too. A turtle has webbed feet to help it swim. A tortoise has short, chubby feet to help it walk.
Can you tell the difference between a turtle and a tortoise?

2 Make a connection.
Write two ways that a turtle and a tortoise are the **same**.
1. ....
2. ....

3 Make a connection.
Write two ways that a turtle and a tortoise are **different**.
1. ....
2. ....

Final blends

Blends are two or three letters that keep their individual sounds when together. Blends can also be found at the end of a word.

These are also called **final blends**.

1) Add the final blend to make each word. Write the word, then draw a picture.

	ld		
Add the blend	chi.ld..	co.......	go.......
Add the word	child	....	....
Draw the picture			

	lt		
Add the blend	me.......	be.......	qui.......
Add the word	....	....	....
Draw the picture			

2 Choose the correct blend for each word.

nk	mp	lk

Try each blend out to see which sounds correct.

la...........

e ....

mi...........

pi...........

wi...........

sta...........

3 Connect the letters to spell the word correctly. Then write the word.

m a nt
b i ng   ...mint...

v nt
a nd   ....

e lk
i lf   ....

4 Read the text. Circle the final blend '**mp**'.

The plump camel has one hump. He cannot jump high, but he is the champ at going far. Don't make him mad, because he can be a grump.

5 How many times did you find the blend '**mp**'?

Fairy tales

A **fairy tale** is a fiction story with magic. Some well-known fairy tales are 'Snow White', 'Jack and the Beanstalk' and 'Goldilocks and the Three Bears'.

1 What is your favourite fairy tale?

....

2 A fairy tale has special details. Write the special details for your favourite fairy tale in the boxes below.

Good characters	Evil characters	Magic

3 Does your favourite fairy tale have a happy ending?

....

Multiple-meaning words

Multiple-meaning words are words that have the same spelling and sound the same but have different meanings.

'**Bark**' is a word that has different meanings. It can mean the sound a dog makes or a part of a tree.

1 Tick the picture that shows the correct meaning of the word in bold.

I posted a **letter**.	The **mouse** ran across the room.	Oh no! The **fly** landed on my food.

○　　　　○	○　　　　○	○　　　　○

2 Read the sentences.
Circle the correct meaning for the word in bold.

a. Every Saturday morning, I **ring** my auntie.

telephone　　　　　　a diamond ring

b. Does wood **sink** or float in water?

go to the bottom　　　　a place to wash your hands

Personal pronouns

We do not always need to use a person's name when we write about them in a sentence.

I, **he**, **she**, **you**, **it**, **we**, **they**, **me**, **him**, **her**, **them** and **us** are words we can use instead of a name.

1 Circle the word that tells us who the sentence is about.

   a. Help me!

   b. How are you?

   c. We like to bake cakes.

   d. The bus driver took them to school.

2 Pick the correct word to complete each sentence.

   a. .... ate the sweets.
     She/Her

Only one word will make sense in each sentence.

   b. .... baked cookies.
     He/Him

   c. Come play with .... !
           us/we

   d. .... went to the sweet shop.
   Them/They

   e. Give it to ....
       I/me

Pronouns

Some **pronouns** tell us who owns something or whose turn it is. **Mine**, **yours**, **ours**, **his**, **hers** and **theirs** tells us about who owns something or whose turn it might be.

1. Choose a word to complete each sentence.

~~yours~~	mine	theirs	ours	hers

a. This is your ball. The ball is .....yours..... .

b. The hat belongs to me. The hat is ....

c. John and Ellen live in that house. The house is ....

d. The girl has a red purse. The purse is ....

e. My family has a black car. The car is ....

2. Circle the correct pronoun for each sentence.

The vanilla milkshake is hers/ours.

The blue camera is his/yours.

Question words

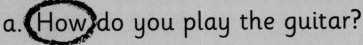

Question words are used to ask a question. **Who**, **what**, **when**, **where**, **why** and **how** are question words.

1 Circle the question words in each sentence.

a. (How) do you play the guitar?

b. When does school start?

c. What did you eat for lunch?

d. Who did that?

e. Where is my dog?

2 Write the correct question word to complete each sentence.

a. .... do you live?

b. .... many days are there until Halloween?

c. .... do you go to bed?

d. .... is your best friend?

e. .... instrument do you play?

Word bank

Who
What
When
Where
How

3 Turn each sentence into a question.

Remember that questions end with a question mark.

a. Layla plays basketball.

Where does Layla play basketball?

b. The rocket is very fast.

....

c. Reagan is feeling sad.

....

d. My next music concert is in May.

....

4 Write a question for each picture.

....
............................?

....
............................?

Ask and answer questions

Key details are important pieces of information in a text. Readers use key details to **ask and answer questions**.

1 Read the text.

Bats are amazing mammals! Did you know that bats are the only mammals that can fly?
They have the best hearing of all land mammals.
Bats make sounds that bounce back to their huge ears.
This is how they find insects to eat. Bats do most of their hunting at night. They are nocturnal.
This means they are awake at night.
During the day, bats sleep hanging upside down with a big group of other bats.

2 Answer these questions.
1. What do bats like to eat? ....
2. When do bats go hunting? ....

3 Tick all the sentences that are true.

☐ Bats stay awake at night.

☐ Bats can hear very well.

☐ Bats can't fly.

4 What else do you want to know about bats? Write one question that you have.

....

....

....?

'A', 'an' and 'the'

'**A**', '**an**' and '**the**' are words we use before a person, place or thing.

Remember, a noun is a person, place or thing.

'**a**' is used before a word that starts with a **consonant**.

'**an**' is used before a word that starts with a **vowel**: '**a**', '**e**', '**i**', '**o**' or '**u**'.

1 Write '**a**' or '**an**' before each word.

...... motorbike ...... bus ...... aeroplane

...... ambulance ...... train ...... submarine

2 Pick the correct word for each sentence.

a	an	the

'**the**' is used before a specific noun.

a. .... fastest train goes 602 kilometres per hour!
b. .... submarine can stay underwater for many months.
c. .... ambulance has special equipment to help sick people.
d. The wind can change the speed of .... hot air balloon.

Digraphs

Digraphs are two letters that make one sound when they are together.

1 Choose the correct digraph '**ch**', '**sh**' or '**th**' to begin each word.

 ch.......

 ....

 ....

 ....

 ....

 ....

2 Say the name of the first picture aloud.
Listen for the digraph sound at the end of the word.
Circle the picture that ends with the same digraph sound.

 bath

 teeth

 hat

 lunch

 sock

 beach

 push

 house

 fish

3 '**Wh**' and '**wr**' are digraphs. Write the correct digraph to complete each word.

 ....ist

 ....ale

 ....istle

 ....ite

4 The digraph '**ph**' sounds like the letter '**f**'.

Read each word and then draw a line to match it to the correct picture.

trophy   dolphin   phone

5 The digraph '**kn**' sounds like the letter '**n**'.
Read the words with the digraph '**kn**' aloud.
Choose the correct word to complete each sentence.

a. You need a fork and .... to cut the pancakes.

b. I have a big .... in my shoelaces.

c. Jessie hurt her .... playing football.

d. The .... was riding a horse.

Word bank

knot
knight
knife
knee

Verbs

A **verb** is an action word. It names something you can do.

Sing, dance and play are all verbs.

1 Read the verbs aloud. Then write the correct verb next to each picture.

drink	eat	~~ride~~	run	climb

..ride.. | .... | .... | .... | ....

2 Circle the verb in each sentence.

a. Mum reads a book.
b. He plays the guitar.
c. I sing a song.
d. We sleep in a tent.
e. Pack your bags.
f. Turn on the torch.

3 What would you do if you went camping?
Write a sentence. Circle the verb in your sentence.

....

....

....

Verb tenses

A **verb** in the **present tense** tells us about an action that is happening **now**.

A **verb** in the **past tense** tells us about an action that has **already happened**.

1 Add '**ed**' to each verb to show that it happened in the past.

Some past tense verbs end with the letters '**ed**'.

Happening now	Happened in the past
cook	cooked
play	
jump	
help	
dance	
shout	

2 Underline the actions that happened in the past in each sentence.

a. We walked in the garden.
b. We planted two trees yesterday.
c. They picked some flowers.
d. The dogs barked and jumped.
e. The cat chased a bee.
f. We looked at the stars in the sky.

Nearly the same

Although some words have **similar meanings**, there are small differences between them.

1 Read the word. Then write a word with a similar meaning.

little ....tiny........   jump ....   cry ....

big ....   cute ....   hug ....

2 Read the three words in each set.
Put them in order from weakest to strongest.

| furious, cross, angry | .... | .... | .... |
| warm, burning, hot | .... | .... | .... |

3 Read the words in the chart.
Then choose two words below with similar meanings.

| ~~gulp~~ | happy | ~~drink~~ |
| excited | sprint | jog |

	Weakest ....▶ Strongest		
sip	drink		gulp
glad			
walk			

Silent 'e'

When 'e' is the final letter in a word, it is usually silent. The other vowel in the word makes its long vowel sound.

Shh!

1 Read the word in the first column. Then make a new word by adding a silent 'e'.

not.......

cap.......

cub.......

bit.......

tub.......

2 Rejig the letters to make a word with a silent 'e'.

m l e i

....

a e p t

....

t e n u

....

e r s o

....

How to

'How to' writing describes the steps needed to do something.

Always ask an adult to help with the blender.

1 Read the smoothie recipe.

How to make a strawberry smoothie

You will need:
400g of strawberries
1 banana
200g of ice
250ml of water
Blender or food processor

Steps:
1. Put the strawberries in the blender.
2. Add the banana.
3. Add the ice to the blender.
4. Pour water over the strawberries, banana and ice.
5. Put the lid on the blender tightly.
6. Turn the blender on high.
7. Blend for one minute or until smooth.

2 Put these steps in order using the numbers 1, 2 or 3.

☐ Add the banana.

☐ Blend for one minute.

☐ Add ice to the blender.

3 Which is not an ingredient to make a strawberry smoothie? Cross it out.

strawberries
apple
banana
ice

4 Think of something that you know how to do.
Write one thing that you could explain to someone.

I can explain how to ....
....
....
....
....
....

5 Write a list of the things you will need to brush your teeth:

You will need:
1. ....
2. ....
3. ....
4. ....

6 Write a list of the steps in order to brush your teeth.
Method:
1. ....
2. ....
3. ....

Long vowel 'a'

The long 'a' sound can be made using 'ay' or 'ai'.

1 Read each word aloud.
Then write each word in the correct egg basket.

hay	lay	rain	ray
play	tail	wait	paid

ai

ay

2 Read the 'ai' and 'ay' words aloud. Find each word in the word search.

- [ ] nail
- [ ] away
- [ ] rainbow
- [ ] day

r	a	i	n	b	o	w
c	y	k	v	i	e	l
n	j	q	h	r	t	a
a	w	f	p	i	e	w
i	u	d	a	y	o	a
l	g	m	s	x	d	y

Long vowel 'e'

The long 'e' sound can be made using 'ee', 'ea' or 'ey'.

How many words can you see with each long 'e' sound?

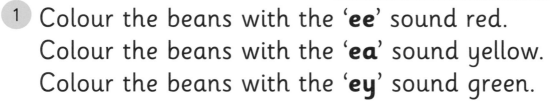

1 Colour the beans with the 'ee' sound red.
Colour the beans with the 'ea' sound yellow.
Colour the beans with the 'ey' sound green.

keep	key	peas	seed	eat
honey	cheek	peach	donkey	clean

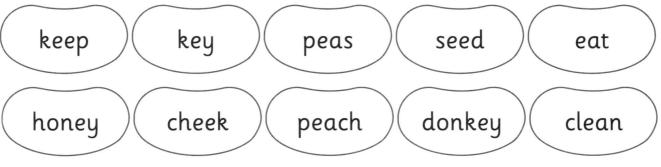

2 Read the words aloud. Add them to the story below.

teeth	treat	green	beans	sweets

I went to the shop to get a ....
My mum said too many .... could hurt
my ....
I got some jelly ....
I like the .... jelly beans the best.

Long vowel 'i'

The long 'i' sound can be made using '**igh**', '**y**' or '**ie**'.

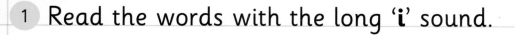

1 Read the words with the long 'i' sound.

tie	sigh	try	sky	cried

fight	night	fries	spy

2 Write each of the words from Activity 1 under the correct long 'i' sound.

pie

1. ....

2. ....

3. ....

Read the example word first to check which long 'i' sound it is.

light

1. ....

2. ....

3. ....

fry

1. ....

2. ....

3. ....

Long vowel 'o'

The long 'o' sound can be made using 'oa', 'oe' or 'ow'.

1 Follow the words in the maze with a long 'o' sound to help the goat get to the toad.

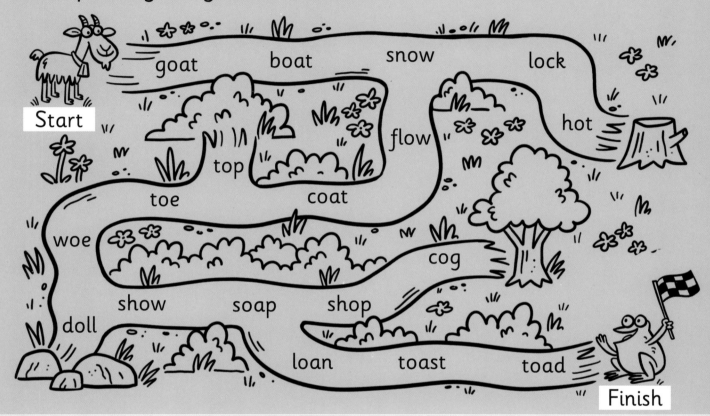

2 Colour the words with the 'ow' sound blue.
Colour the words with the 'oa' sound green.
Colour the words with the 'oe' sound orange.

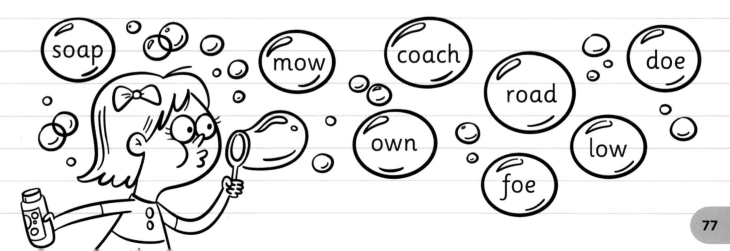

Long vowel 'u'

The long 'u' sound can be made using 'ew', 'ue' or 'ui'.

1 Tick each of the words with the correct long 'u' spelling.

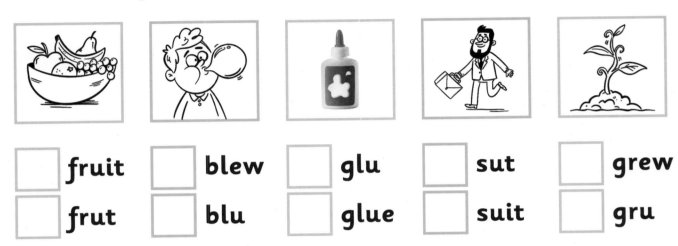

☐ fruit   ☐ blew   ☐ glu   ☐ sut   ☐ grew
☐ frut   ☐ blu   ☐ glue   ☐ suit   ☐ gru

2 Read the words aloud.
Write the correct word next to each definition.

chew   clue   cruise

a. A trip on a large boat. ....
b. To make food smaller using your teeth. ....
c. A hint that helps solve the problem. ....

3 Read the sentences. Circle all the words with a long 'u' sound.

Each sentence has more than one!

a. The blue plane flew over the ocean.
b. I have a few books due to the library.
c. I wish I knew how to make stew.

Long vowels

Go to page 101 to read more about split digraphs.

1 Spell the word using the correct split digraph.

a-e	o-e	i-e	u-e

.........mute.........

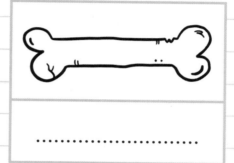

....

....

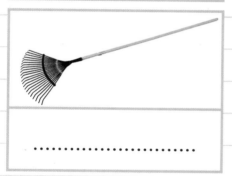

....

....

....

2 Read the words aloud and listen for a long vowel sound. Cross out the word in each row that does not have a long vowel sound.

Long 'a'	cute	wait	cave	day
Long 'e'	need	mean	Pete	ripe
Long 'i'	lorry	time	high	lie
Long 'o'	know	vote	luck	loaf
Long 'u'	juice	chew	use	lamp

Time words

Time words tell us when something happened. **First**, **next**, **then**, **last** and **finally** tell us when things happened in a story.

1 Draw a line from each word or phrase to the part of a story where it would be used.

first   beginning   finally

last   middle   next

then   at the end

end

in the beginning   once upon a time

2 Fill in numbers 1, 2 or 3 to put the story of Drake Dragon in order.

☐ **Then** Drake asked his mum for help.
☐ **After** his mum helped him, Drake could fly.
☐ The **first** time Drake tried to fly, he fell to the ground.

3 Fill in numbers 1, 2, 3 or 4 to put the story of Uma Unicorn in order.

☐ **Next**, she played with her friends.
☐ **One day**, Uma Unicorn went for a walk.
☐ **Finally**, Uma Unicorn ate dinner and went to sleep.
☐ **After** playing for a long time, Uma went home.

Using time words

Writers use **time words** to share their ideas in order.

Think about your favourite day.

1. **What are three things that happened that day?**

   My favourite day was my birthday party!

   1. ....

   2. ....

   3. ....

2. Write a story about your day using **first**, **then** and **finally** for the beginning, middle and end of the story.

First...

Then...

Finally...

Syllables

'**Apple**' has two syllables. Clap twice as you say the word.

Words can be broken into parts called **syllables**. You can clap to count the syllables in a word.

1 Read each word aloud. Clap the number of syllables.

1 syllable		2 syllables		3 syllables	
owl	bat	penguin	turtle	crocodile	koala

2 Read each word aloud and clap the number of syllables. Circle the correct number of syllables for each word.

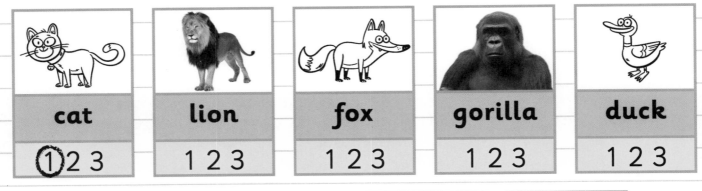

cat	lion	fox	gorilla	duck
①2 3	1 2 3	1 2 3	1 2 3	1 2 3

rabbit	giraffe	fly	parrot
1 2 3	1 2 3	1 2 3	1 2 3

3 Read each word aloud and clap for each syllable. Write the word in the correct column.

map	camel	deer	zookeeper
monkey	elephant	bear	panda

1 syllable	2 syllables	3 syllables
1.	1.	1. ....
2.	2.	2. ....
3.	3.	

4 Clap then write the number of syllables in each word. Following the example, draw a line to break the written words into syllables.

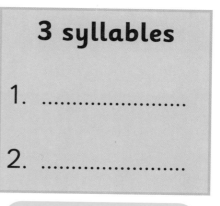

Words with one syllable do not need to be broken into parts.

	Number of syllables	Show syllables
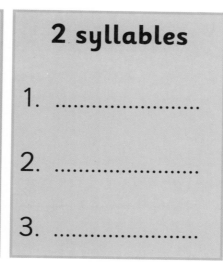	...........2...........	ti/g e r
	....	s l o t h
	....	f l a m i n g o

Long or short vowels

Vowels can make many sounds, including long and short sounds.

For example, '**can**' has a short vowel and '**cane**' has a long vowel.

1. Say each word aloud. Does it have a long or short vowel sound? Circle the correct answer.

June	**plan**	**show**	**meat**	**end**
(long) short	long short	long short	long short	long short

tray	**slime**	**duck**	**trim**	**blob**
long short	long short	long short	long short	long short

2. Colour the words with a long vowel sound yellow. Colour the words with a short vowel sound blue.

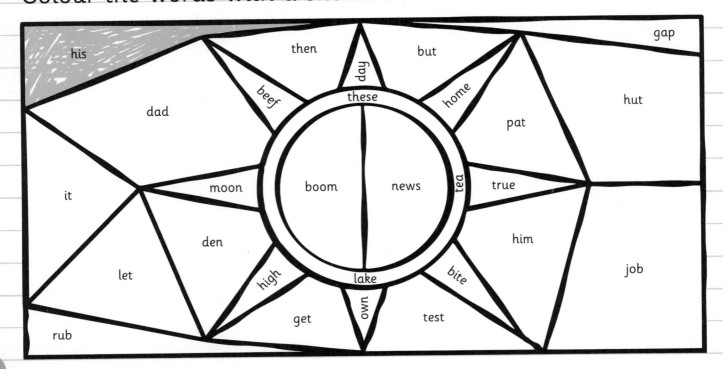

The letter 'y'

The letter '**y**' is a consonant but can sometimes act like a vowel. When '**y**' is used like a vowel, it makes the **long /e/** sound like in the word '**happy**' or the **long /i/** sound like in the word '**by**'.

1. If the letter '**y**' sounds like **long /e/** colour the leaf green.
   If the letter '**y**' sounds like **long /i/** colour the leaf red.
   If the letter '**y**' sounds like **consonant /y/** colour the leaf orange.

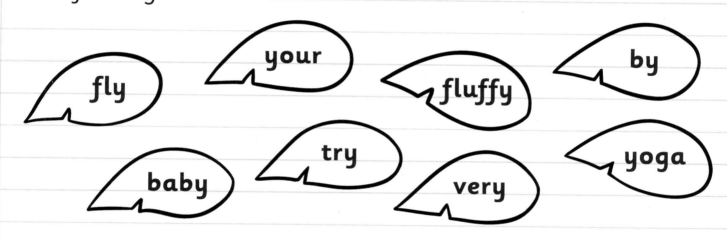

2. Sort each word into the correct group.

sky	yes	lucky	tiny	cry	yet

Sounds like long 'e'	Sounds like long 'i'	Sounds like consonant 'y'
....	....	....
....	....	....

Singular and plural nouns

Singular means one person, place or thing.

Plural means more than one person, place or thing.

1 Colour the words that describe one thing red.
Colour the words that describe more than one thing blue.

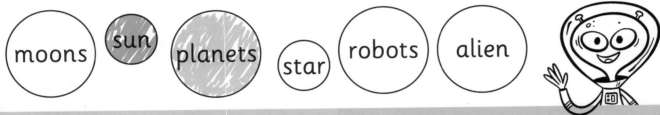

moons sun planets star robots alien

2 Many nouns can be made plural by adding an '**s**' to the end of the word. Make the nouns plural by adding '**s**'.

Singular	Plural
satellite	satellites
bed	....
rocket	....
helmet	....
girl	....

3 Some nouns are made plural by adding '**es**' to the end of the word. Make the nouns plural by adding '**es**'.

Singular	Plural
dish	dishes
torch	....
glass	....
box	....
brush	....

Nouns that end in '**ch**', '**sh**', '**s**', or '**z**' need an '**es**' at the end.

Nouns and verbs

When a noun is **plural**, the verb that comes after it does not end in '**s**'.

When a noun is **singular**, the verb that comes after it ends in '**s**'.

1 Circle the correct verb for each sentence.

a. The monsters (**eat**/eats) crisps.

For example: The **ball rolls** down the hill.

b. A troll (live/lives) under the bridge.

c. Dragons (stay/stays) near the castle.

d. The witch (make/makes) a potion.

e. A toad (sing/sings) a song.

f. Mermaids (swim/swims) in the ocean.

2 Write a sentence about a friendly monster who has a football. Choose the correct verb to use in your sentence.

| play | plays |

Is the noun singular or plural?

....

....

....

Finding clues

1. Use the other words in the sentence to figure out the meaning of the bold word. Circle the correct meaning.

   a. She is feeling **drowsy** because she stayed up late.

   | **sleepy** or **happy** |

   b. After lunch, the children quickly **dash** to the playground.

   | **run** or **wait** |

   c. I walked **briskly** to catch up to my sister.

   | **quickly** or **slowly** |

2. Read the sentence and look at the picture. Find clues to work out the meaning of the word in bold. Write the meaning of the word below.

   Joseph was so cold that his body started to **shiver**.

   Use the picture to help!

Shiver means ....

3 Read the text.

Mummy Squirrel had a problem, so she asked Ruby Rabbit for help. She told Ruby that Little Squirrel was **missing**. "When was the last time you saw him?" Ruby asked.

"I saw him this morning. We were looking for nuts. Then I **hurried** home, but he stayed out to play," Mummy Squirrel said.

Ruby went to find out more. She looked until she found Little Squirrel's paw prints. Oh no! Little Squirrel was stuck in the mud. Ruby pulled him out and took him home to Mummy Squirrel. "Thank you!" Mummy Squirrel said.

Little Squirrel and Mummy Squirrel were **delighted** to be together again.

4 Use the text above to answer the questions.

Find each difficult word in the story and reread the sentence. Swap the word with your answer to see if it makes sense.

1. What does the word **missing** mean?

   lost   asked

2. What does the word **hurried** mean?

   rushed   sleep

3. What does the word **delighted** mean?

   scared   happy

Make an inference

Readers **make an inference** when they use what they already know and clues in the text to figure out something.

It is important to make inferences because authors don't always tell the reader everything they need to know.

1 Read the sentence. Decide which answer matches it.

1. José bought a tent, a sleeping bag and a fishing rod.
   ○ He is going to play football.
   ○ He is going camping.

2. Rex has a party hat on his head.
   ○ It is Rex's birthday.
   ○ It is Rex's first day of school.

3. There are dark clouds in the sky.
   ○ It is a sunny day.
   ○ It is about to rain.

4. The dog has a stick in his mouth.
   ○ The dog wants to play fetch.
   ○ The dog wants to go to sleep.

Position

Some words help us to know where something is, or what **position** it is in. **On**, **beside** and **in front of** tell us where something is.

1 Help complete the treasure map by following the directions below. Pay close attention to the position words in bold.

∧∧∧ Draw three shark fins **in** the ocean.

⛄⛄ Draw trees **next to** Alligator Swamp.

✗ Put an ✗ **between** the mountains.

Add a treasure chest **under** the ✗.

≈≈≈ Draw a river **above** the mountains.

Alligator Swamp

N

S

Pirate Ocean

3-letter blends

Blends are two or three letters that are often found together in words. Each letter keeps its own sound when you sound out the word.

Say each word aloud first.

1 Circle the correct 3-letter blend.

	str squ		spr squ		scr str
	str squ	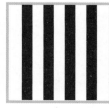	scr str		scr squ
	spr scr		spr squ		spl spr

2 Write the correct word next to its definition.

stretch	**spread**	**splinter**	**scroll**

a. A way to move your body. ....

b. How to put jam on bread. ....

c. A small piece of wood in your finger. ....

d. A roll of paper from long ago. ....

3 Complete the crossword puzzle by filling in the missing
3-letter blends to complete each word.

| str | scr | squ | thr | spr | spl |

Cross out the
blends as you go!

4 Write two sentences choosing one word with a
3-letter blend from Activity 3.

1. ....
....
2. ....
....

Plan a non-fiction text

Writers think about ideas before choosing what to write about.

1 Write a list of animals that you might like to write about.

....
....
....
....
....
....

2 Now circle the animal you would like to write about. This will be your topic for Activity 3.

3 Writers research their topics. Write the answers to the questions that you already know. Then ask an adult to help you research the other answers.

To research means to find out more about something.

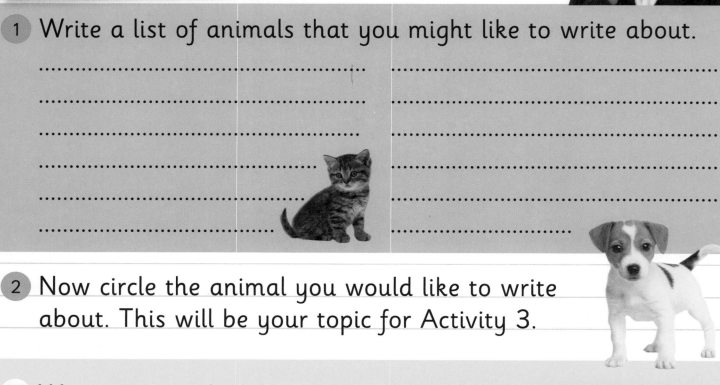

What is the animal's name?..

What does it look like?..

What does it eat?..

Where does it live?..

94

Write a non-fiction text

The first sentence tells the reader what you are writing about.

1. Use your research from the previous page to write five sentences about your animal.

   1. ....
   ....

   2. ....
   ....

   3. ....
   ....

   4. ....
   ....

   5. ....
   ....

2. Draw a picture of your animal.

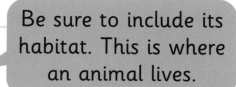

Be sure to include its habitat. This is where an animal lives.

Which letter is saying its name?

When the letter 'r' comes after a vowel, it changes the sound the vowel makes.

This is sometimes called **Bossy R** because the 'r' says its name such as '**park**'.

1 Read the '**ar**' words aloud.
   Complete each sentence with the correct '**ar**' word.

shark	farm	star	bark

1. Cherry the dog has a loud ....

2. An ocean is home for a ....

3. Did you know that the sun is a ....?

4. The pigs live on the ....

2 Draw a line from each '**or**' word to the correct picture.

corn	north	fork

3 Draw a line from each 'er' word to the correct picture.

butter	tiger	person	hammer

In some words, 'er', 'ir' and 'ur' make the same sound.

4 Read the text. Highlight the words with 'ir' in yellow. Then write the 'ir' words below.

"Chirp," said the bird.
He looked in the dirt for food.
The girl in a skirt let him eat from her birdhouse.

1. ....

2. ....

3. ....

4. ....

5. ....

6. ....

5 Add 'ur' to each word in the sentence. Then draw a picture to match.

The n........se has c........ly p........ple hair.

Compound words

A **compound word** is when two words are put together to make a different word.

Some compound words are **inside**, **blueberry** and **cowboy**.

1. Make a compound word using one of the words below.

book	corn	ring

	pop	+	....	=	....
	note	+	....	=	....
	ear	+	....	=	....

2. Circle the compound word that solves each riddle.

a. I live in the ocean. I am pretty to see. Some even say I sting like a bee.

starfish	jellyfish	shellfish

b. To see me, you need to look up high. My seven colours fill the sky.

raincoat	raindrop	rainbow

Point of view

Point of view is the view from which a story is told. A story can be told by the author, a character or a narrator.

> A **narrator** is a storyteller who is not a character in the story.

1 Read about the different points of view.

Point of view	Who is telling the story
Character's point of view	The story is told by one of the characters.
Author's point of view	The story is told by the author of the text. The author speaks to the reader.
Narrator's point of view	The story is told by a narrator who is not part of the story.

2 Read the sentences. Decide if it is the narrator or the character in the story telling us each sentence.

> Find clues in the sentence to help you select the point of view.

I am so excited to go to the woods tomorrow.	**character/narrator**
The fairies were so happy that they hugged each other tightly.	**character/narrator**
What is happening to us?	**character/narrator**

Author's point

The **author** writes the story. Sometimes authors have a special message that they are trying to share with us.

1 Olivia wrote about homework. Read her writing.

> ### No Homework by Olivia
>
> Kids should not have to do homework. When we get home, we need to spend time with family. We also need time to do other things like sports and music. Grown-ups do not have to do homework. That is not fair. These are the reasons kids should not have to do homework.

2 Answer these questions.

1. Who is the author? ....

2. What is the main message in their writing? ....
....
....

3. Why does the author think children should not have to do homework? ....
....
....

4. Do you agree with the author? ....
....
Why? ....
....
....

Split digraphs

Split digraphs are two letters that are separated by another letter. They are '**a-e**', '**e-e**', '**i-e**', '**o-e**' and '**u-e**'.

The first letter in a split digraph says its name when we are reading it in a word. For example:

The k**i**t**e** flew as high as the cr**a**n**e**.

The word '**kite**' has the '**i-e**' split digraph so says the letter '**i**'. The word '**crane**' has the '**a-e**' split digraph so says the letter '**a**'.

① Colour the '**o-e**' words **yellow**.
Colour the '**a-e**' words **red**.
Colour the '**u-e**' words **blue**.

Remember, the first letter in a split digraph says its name.

hose	cake	stone	flute

snake	cube	cute	rose

② Use '**i-e**' or '**e-e**' to complete each word.

del.....t.....	k.....t.....	l.....k.....

n.....n.....	th.....m.....	l.....m.....

Joining words

Some words can be used to **join** two sentences or phrases such as **but**, **or**, **so**, **and**, **because**.

1 Connect the words using the joining word.
Write the phrase on the line.

and

| in | out |

.... in and out ....

| noughts | crosses |

....

| this | that |

....

or

| right | wrong |

....

| hot | cold |

....

| truth | dare |

....

2 Say each joining word aloud.
Complete each sentence by filling the gap.

a. We like to play go fish .... snap.

b. You might win .... lose.

c. Jason wants to finish the puzzle, ... there is a missing piece.

Word bank
but
and
or

3 Read the text. Underline the joining words.

> The music played and we walked around the chairs.
> There were two of us but only one chair.
> The music stopped, so we stopped walking.
> I sat down because I was near to the chair. Hurray! I won!

4 Write the joining words that you underlined.

1. ....

2. ....

3. ....

4. ....

Remember:
but, **or**, **so**, **and**,
because are all
joining words.

5 Pick a joining word to complete each sentence.

a. We should play more games at school
   but/because games are fun.

b. Video games help kids learn **so/and**
   find out new things.

c. Hide-and-seek is fun to play **but/or**
   you need lots of players.

Extended sentences

An **extended sentence** is when two or more sentences are combined with a joining word.

Here is an extended sentence:

I like the colour red	but	orange is my favourite colour.
1st sentence	joining word	2nd sentence

1. Read each pair of sentences.
Draw a circle around the compound sentence in each pair.

a. I like to go to the library.
I like to go to the library and I read books there.

b. The vet takes care of my dog.
The vet takes care of my dog and she gives him medicine.

c. The market is open today but it will be closed tomorrow.
The market is closed tomorrow.

2. Make an extended sentence by joining the sentences together.

The second sentence starts with a lowercase letter when sentences are combined.

a. I went to the dentist. I got a new toothbrush.
.... and ....

b. I wanted a new book. The library was closed.
.... but ....

Tricky words

Many **tricky words** have irregular spellings. These words are not spelled like they sound. That is one reason why we learn them off by heart.

1 Read the tricky words.
Write the correct word to complete each sentence.

great	busy	laugh	was

a. Your jokes make me ....
b. We were very ....working in the garden.
c. Harvey had a .... time dancing with his friends.
d. The apple .... sweet and juicy.

2 Practise spelling and writing each tricky word.

Say the word	Spell the word	Write the word
great	g-r-e-a-t	
busy	b-u-s-y	
laugh	l-a-u-g-h	
was	w-a-s	

Root words

A **root word** is a word that can stand alone. A root word can be changed by adding letters to the beginning or the end of the word.

1 Find and highlight the root word in yellow.

Base word	Highlight the root word	
wash	washing	rewash
play	playful	playing
hope	hoped	hopeful
call	recalled	calling
ring	ringing	rings
new	newest	renew

2 Draw a line to match each word to its base word.

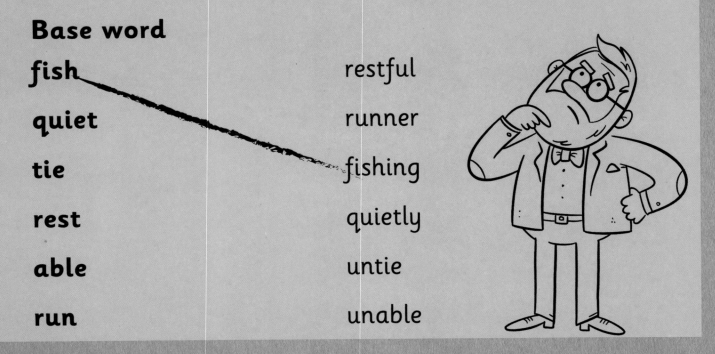

Base word

fish   restful

quiet   runner

tie   fishing

rest   quietly

able   untie

run   unable

Suffixes

Suffixes are letters added to the end of words. To add '**ed**' means something has already happened. To add '**ing**' means something is happening now. By adding '**ed**' or '**ing**' you change a word's meaning.

1. Fill in the chart. Read each word aloud.

Base word	Add 'ed' Past tense	Add 'ing' Present tense
cook	cooked	cooking
jump		
talk		
clean		

2. The word ending '**ed**' can have many sounds.
It can sound like /**t**/ in 'looked'.
It can sound like /**d**/ in 'played'.
It can sound like /**id**/ in 'wanted'.
Read the word. Tick the sound that you hear for '**ed**'.

fixed	/t/	/d/	/id/
loved	/t/	/d/	/id/
wanted	/t/	/d/	/id/
closed	/t/	/d/	/id/
waited	/t/	/d/	/id/
worked	/t/	/d/	/id/

'Er', 'est'

We can add '**er**' and '**est**' to describing words to help them tell us even more about what they are describing.

1 Add '**er**' to each word.

sharp.........   cold.........   long.........

2 Use the '**er**' words from Activity 1 to fill in the gaps.

a. My milkshake was cold but the ice-cream was much ....

b. The nail is .... than the scissors.

c. Mei's hair is .... than Ella's hair.

3 Add '**est**' to each word.

slow...........

hard...........

warm...........

4 Following the example, fill in the missing words to complete each sequence.

a. big, bigger, ...biggest....
b. hard, ..., hardest
c. slow, slower, ...

'Tch'

'**Tch**' is a trigraph. Trigraphs are groups of 3 letters that make a sound when put together.

We use '**tch**' after short vowels like '**a**' in cat, '**u**' in hut, or '**i**' in wit.

1 Complete each word by adding '**tch**'.
Then match the words to the pictures.

fe**tch**   pi............   wa............   ca............

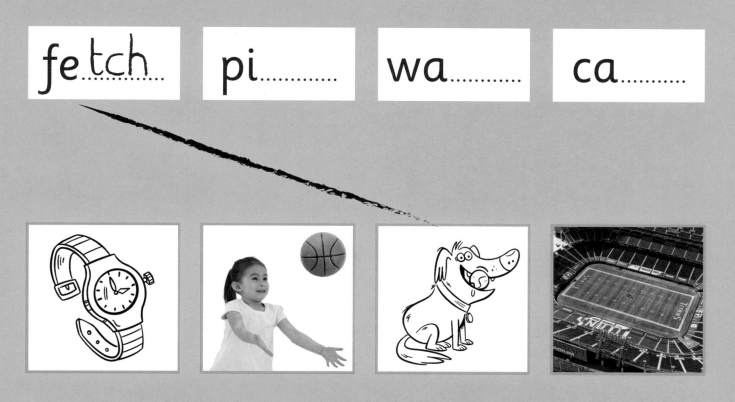

2 Read the words aloud. Cross out the nonsense words.

switch	lotch	bomtch	ditch	fintch
zaptch	hutch	gulltch	crutch	witch

'Air' and 'ear'

'**Air**' and '**ear**' are trigraphs. Trigraphs are groups of 3 letters that make a sound when put together.

1 Fill in the correct trigraph to complete each word.

ear
n.................
f.................
y.................

air
unf.................
ch.................
l.................

2 Choose '**air**' or '**ear**' to complete the word that matches the picture.

b................d

h................y

3 Pick a letter to complete each word.

........airy

i	f	p

........ear

o	z	d

s........air

r	t	e

Prefixes and suffixes

Prefixes are groups of letters that can be added to the **beginning** of a word to change its meaning. **Suffixes** are groups of letters that are added to the **end** of a word to change its meaning.

1 Do these words have a prefix or a suffix? Tick the correct answer.

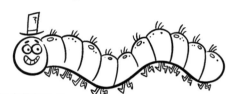

remove	prefix	◯	suffix	◯
singer	prefix	◯	suffix	◯
teacher	prefix	◯	suffix	◯
preschool	prefix	◯	suffix	◯

2 The words below have a prefix or a suffix.
Circle the words that have a prefix.
Underline the words with a suffix.

player	**pretest**	**farmer**	**kindness**	**precook**
unsafe	**seller**	**rename**	**retell**	**fastest**

3 These words have the same suffix: farm**er**, teach**er**, play**er**, sing**er**. Write two more words with the suffix '**er**'.

1. ....

Remember, suffixes go at the end of a word.

2. ....

Make a timeline

A **timeline** shows important events in order by date.

A timeline can use years, months, days or hours.

1   Mae Jemison has been a doctor and an astronaut. Read the timeline about Mae Jemison's life.

Mae Jemison was born.

She graduated from high school.

Mae Jemison became a doctor.

She took her first trip into space.

1956   1973   1981   1992

2   Make a timeline about your life. Write important events and the year they happened on the timeline.

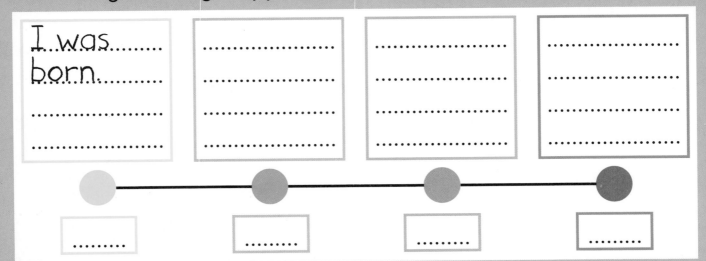

I was born.

Plan a narrative

A **narrative** tells a story. Writers make a plan before they write a story.

1. Think of something you did that was exciting or difficult. Make a list of those things.

1. ....

2. ....

3. ....

Circle the idea that you like best. This is the topic for your narrative.

2. Plan for your story. Answer each of the questions using words or phrases.

Who was there?
....
....
....
....

Where and when did it happen?
....
....
....

What were your feelings?
....
....
....
....

What happened in the beginning?
....
....
....

What happened in the middle?
....
....
....

What happened in the end?
....
....
....

Make a draft

Writers will often make a first **draft**. The first draft does not have to be perfect; it is the first version of your story. You will make it better later.

Remember to use time words like '**next**' and '**then**'.

1 Write the first draft of your story. Use your notes from the previous page to help you.

2 Read your story aloud. Follow the steps below to revise and edit your work.

1. Make sure each sentence starts with a capital letter.
2. Make sure each sentence ends with the correct punctuation mark.
3. Circle the tricky words. Get help from an adult to fix the spelling of the tricky words.
4. Reread the story. Fix any parts that do not make sense.

Write a narrative

Writers make a **final version** of their stories to share with others.

1 Write the final version of your story. Make sure you include any changes that you made to make it better.

2 Draw a picture for your story.

Write an opinion

An **opinion** tells what you think or how you feel about a topic. People have different opinions.

1 Gloria thinks that pineapples are the best fruit. Read her opinion below.

The Best Dessert by Gloria

I think pineapples are the best fruit. Pineapples are the best because they are so sweet. They taste good as juice too. Pineapples can be eaten for dessert. That is why yummy pineapples are the best!

2 What is the best dessert? Share your opinion by responding below.

The best dessert is

....

It is the best because

....

....

....

3 Draw a picture of your favourite dessert.

Write a letter

A **letter** is a written message usually sent in the post.

A pen pal is a person you get to know by writing letters.

1 Read the letter below.

> Dear human,
>
> Greetings from the planet Splog! My name is Glug and I am six years old. My planet is very pretty. There are lots of purple brees. What colour are the brees on your planet?
>
> I live with my mum and grandad in Splogville. We like to go fishing for flugs and weets. Yummy!
>
> From, Scrup

2 Can you write a letter back to Scrup telling the alien all about yourself?

> Dear ....,
>
> I live in ....
> I live with ....
> My family likes to ....
> ....
> ....
> From, ...
>
> Your name

Answers

Page 4-5

Page 6-7

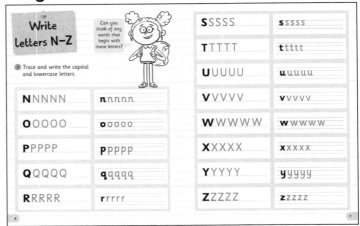

Page 8-9

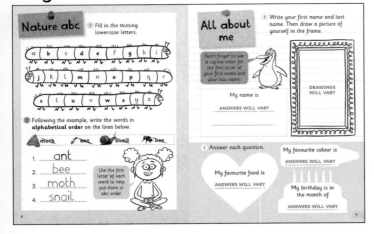

Page 10-11

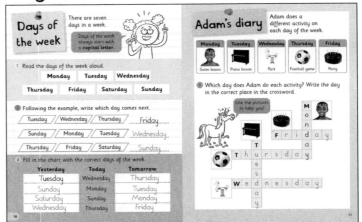

Page 12-13

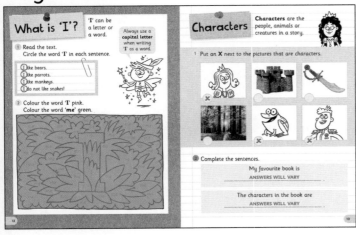

Page 14-15

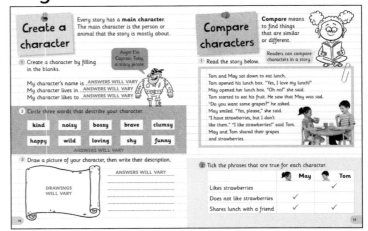

Page 16-17

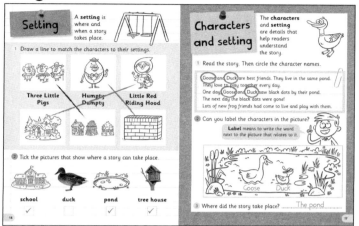

Page 18-19

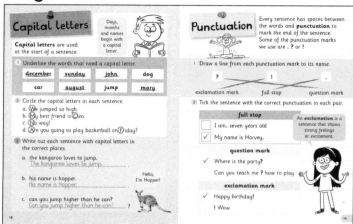

Page 20-21

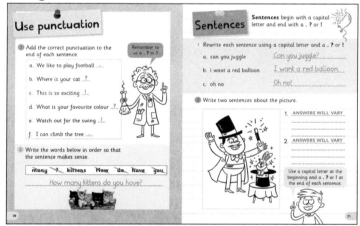

Page 22-23

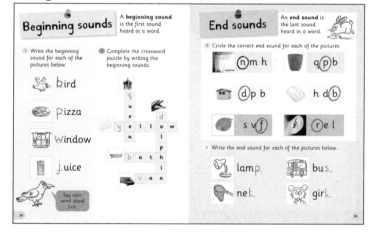

Page 24-25

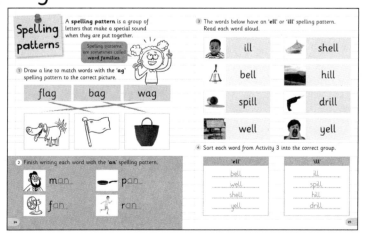

Page 26-27

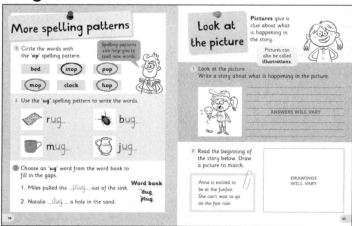

Answers

Page 28-29

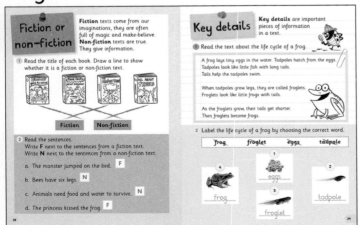

Page 30-31

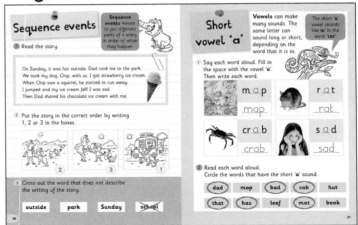

Page 32-33

Page 34-35

Page 36-37

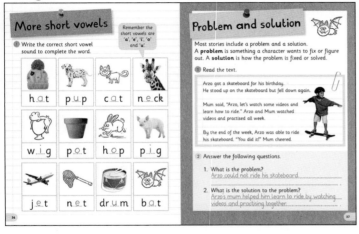

Page 38-39

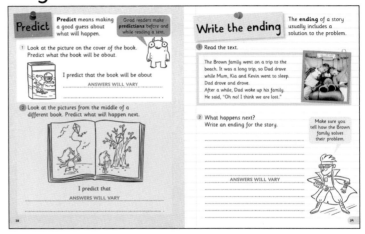

Page 40-41

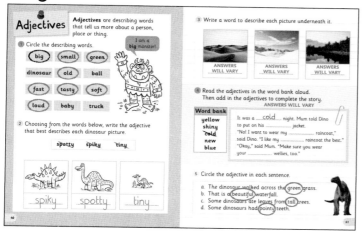

Page 42-43

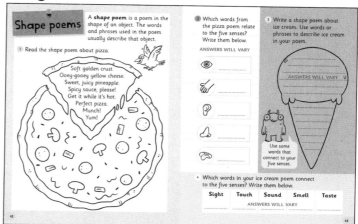

Page 44-45

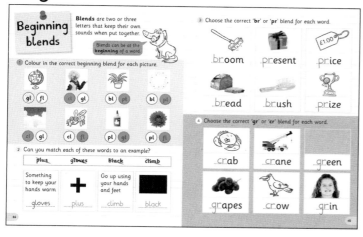

Page 46-47

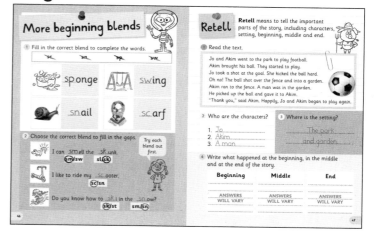

Page 48-49

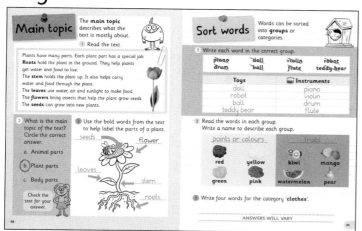

Page 50-51

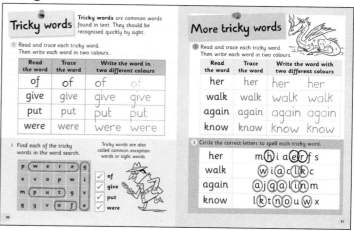

Answers

Page 52-53

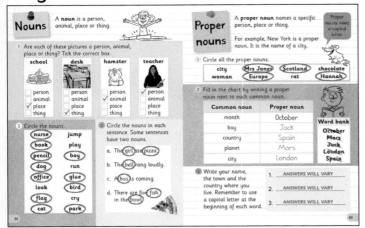

Page 54-55

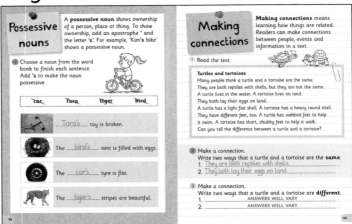

Page 56-57

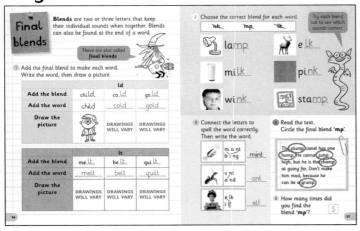

Page 58-59

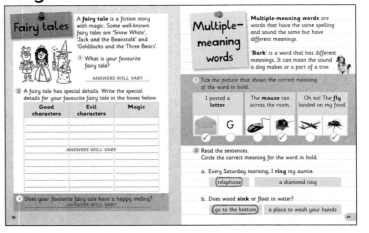

Page 60-61

Page 62-63

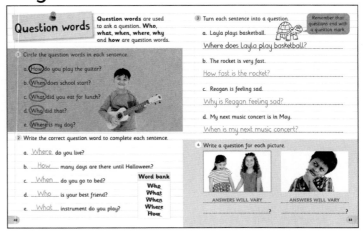

Page 64-65

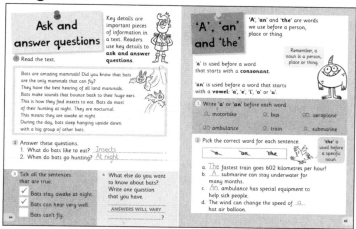

Page 66-67

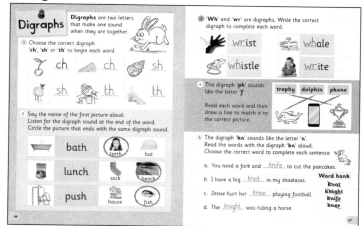

Page 68-69

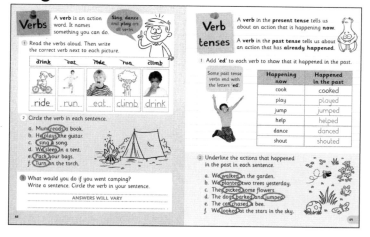

Page 70-71

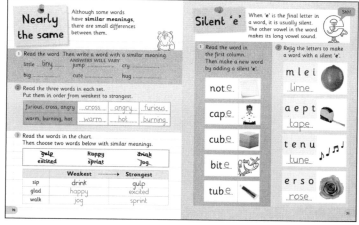

Page 72-73

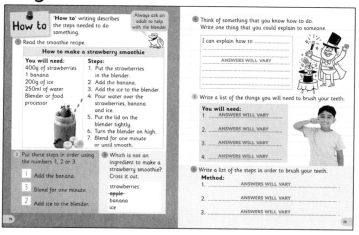

Page 74-75

Answers

Page 76-77

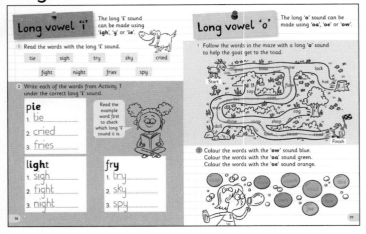

Page 78-79

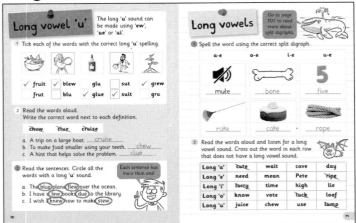

Page 80-81

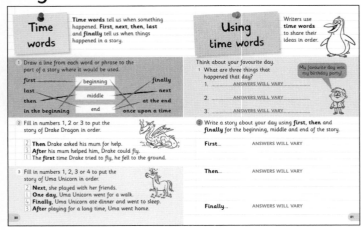

Page 82-83

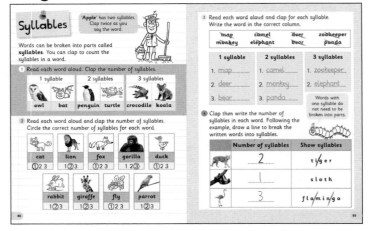

Page 84-85

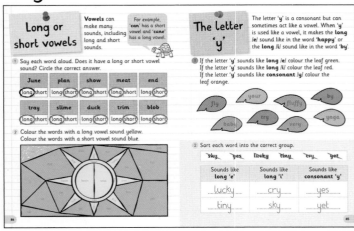

Page 86-87

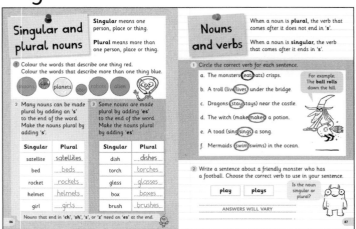

Page 88-89

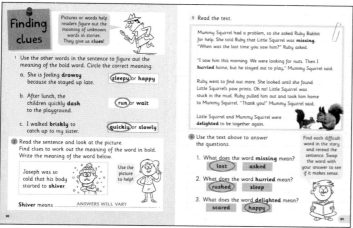

Page 90-91

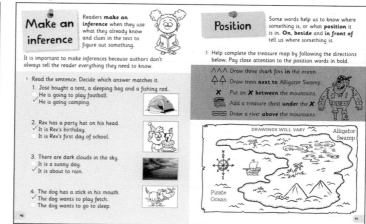

Page 92-93

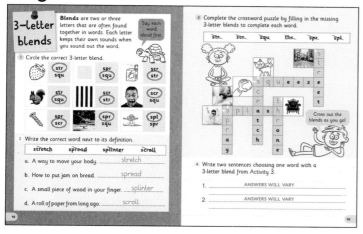

Page 94-95

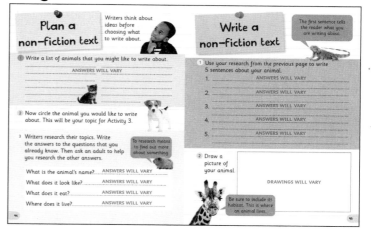

Page 96-97

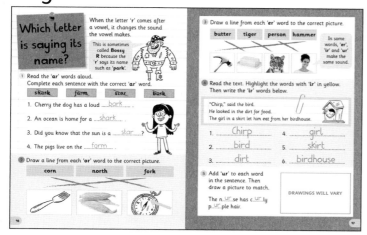

Page 98-99

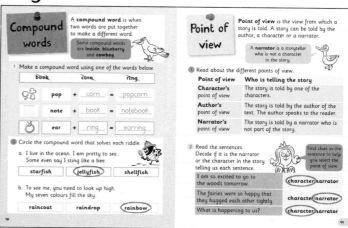

Answers

Page 100-101

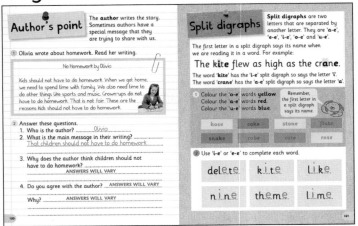

Page 102-103

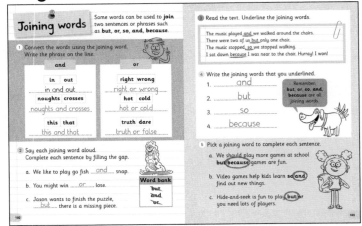

Page 104-105

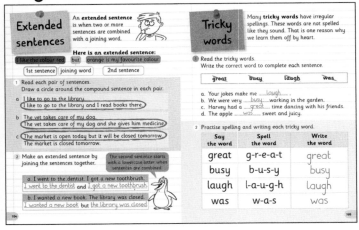

Page 106-107

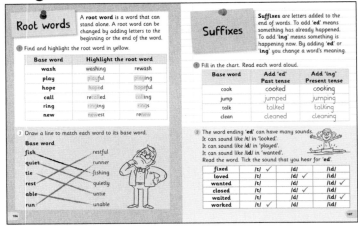

Page 108-109

Page 110-111

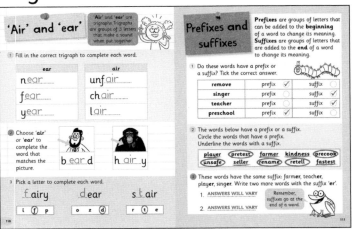

Page 112-113

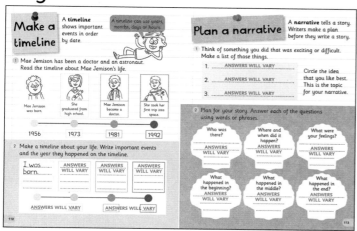

Page 114-115

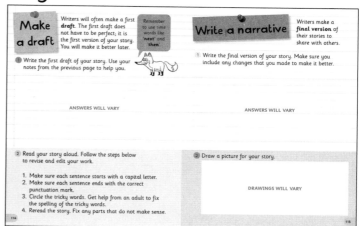

Page 116-117

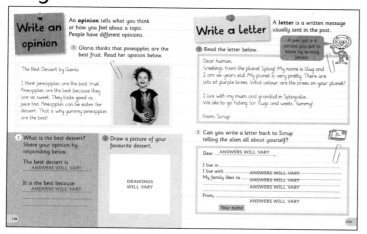

Credits

Educational Consultants: Kimberley Burnim & Ciara O'Connor, BEd, MA
Editors: Alice-May Bermingham & Natalie Munday
Senior Designer: Rhea Gaughan
Designers: Nic Davies & Alice Baird
Production Controller: Rosie Cunniffe
Illustrator: Lee Cosgrove